NE

DROP ^THE **GOAL**

NEVER MIND
THE
DROP GOAL

The Unofficial
RUGBY
WORLD CUP

QUIZ BOOK

PHIL ASCOUGH
Foreword by JASON LEONARD

The
History
Press

First published 2015

The History Press
The Mill, Brimscombe Port
Stroud, Gloucestershire, GL5 2QG
www.thehistorypress.co.uk

British Library Cataloguing in Publication Data.
A catalogue record for this book is available from the British Library.

ISBN 978 0 7509 6283 4

Typesetting and origination by The History Press
Printed in Great Britain

Contents

Foreword
by Jason Leonard

Making my England debut at the age of 22, against Argentina in 1990, it would have been hard to contemplate ever having the chances to create the career I experienced during those fourteen years of pulling on that England jersey and the opportunities it has afforded me post-retirement.

With 114 caps for England and three tours with the British and Irish Lions, I was lucky enough to not only play in the biggest games in world rugby but to also be part of the winning side on plenty of grand occasions. Through sport you will always get the predictable knocks and strains of a front row rugby player, including a broken vertebra in the 1992 Five Nations. However, those times in rugby make you appreciate the support that the game has for all players, managers, fans and the spirit to help others. Recovery was easier and, of course, it made the winning Lions tour of South Africa in 1997 and the 2003 Rugby World Cup triumph that much sweeter.

There are not many occasions when I am not asked about that night in Sydney in 2003. The full-time whistle brought an overwhelming feeling of happiness and pride. Jonny Wilkinson's kick in the last 26 seconds of extra time changed England rugby history forever and it is a moment that I will never forget.

That World Cup final win added to another honour that brings me immense pride: England rugby's most-capped player. On 114 different occasions I stepped on to that field to do my country proud.

Perhaps remembered most by the public for my international career, my club career, which spanned both the amateur and professional eras of rugby, allowed me to represent great clubs – initially Barking and then the rugby domestic Goliaths that are Saracens and Harlequins. A brief stint at Saracens introduced me to top-level rugby and allowed the move to Harlequins, where I would stay for the rest of my career, completing 183 appearances for the club and ending on a high with the European Parker Pen Challenge Cup win in May 2004.

Having been involved in charity work, including roles as lead ambassador of the Wooden Spoon Society and president of the Sparks charity, it is with great pleasure that I am now in a position to launch the Atlas Foundation. The Atlas Foundation will provide the financial support to worldwide charities that use the game of rugby as a facilitator to improve the lives of underprivileged people. These rugby-based charities face an enduring problem funding their activities. As an independent charity funded through sponsorship, our fundraising and donations will allow such causes to focus on delivery. By seeking out and securing tailored grant funding from large UK corporations and matching donations to charitable organisations, the Foundation will advance and promote the efficiency of rugby-based charities around the world. Our work will allow them to apply their resources in a more effective manner towards carrying out their charitable purposes.

It gives me further pleasure that, in the true philanthropic and charitable nature of the game of rugby, Phil has offered his support to the Atlas Foundation by contributing proceeds from this book.

Jason Leonard played 114 Test matches for England between 1990 and 2004, and also played six Tests for the British and Irish Lions among a total of twenty-four appearances during three Lions tours. Jason was a member of the England side who won the Rugby World Cup in 2003, and his total of twenty-two appearances in four editions of the tournament remains a record. He was appointed president of the Rugby Football Union for 2015. To find out more about Jason's work with the Atlas Foundation please call 0844 880 40333 or email enquiries@sporting-vision.co.uk.

Introduction

The admission that a rugby club taught me how to drink will, undoubtedly, strike a chord with many people.

It was years ago – long before the club evolved into Doncaster Knights and back in an age of drunken nights, messy nights and I'll-be-in-big-trouble-when-I-get-home nights.

It was also more than a decade before the advent of the Rugby World Cup, these days a giant of a tournament, which has harnessed the poise, pace and power of the players, and the commercial nous of the organisers to claim a place as one of the great global sporting events.

Naturally enough, my most treasured memory of the Rugby World Cup is the commentary from 2003, which for many people defined Ian Robertson's broadcasting career: '… and there's no time for Australia to come back!' It's spine-tingling stuff, even now.

A close second, though was 1991, not because England were in the final but because of where I watched it: Bermuda. Living in Bermuda, it was possible to watch English Premier League football live on TV in the morning and then spend the afternoon at the club where the island's four rugby teams contested their championship. In such an environment the sport was even more sociable than back in England as Bermudians, Brits, Americans,

10

Canadians and more traded blows on the pitch, and then beer or Black Seal Rum in the bar.

But Bermuda really makes its mark in the world of sport with its Rugby Classics. Guest players at one Easter Classic included David Campese and Jeremy Guscott, who contributed to a points total of more than 100 in a scintillating display of festival rugby, although that event was merely a potboiler for the World Rugby Classic.

Introduced in 1988 and styling itself as 'The Scrum of the Earth', the World Rugby Classic is veterans' rugby at its best and has featured some legends of the game. The website, at www.worldrugby.bm, carries testimonials from such luminaries as Guscott, Willie John McBride and François Pienaar. Oh – and Hollywood superstar Michael Douglas.

In those days, the notion of a team like Bermuda taking part in a Rugby World Cup was the stuff of fantasy. That the nation is now part of the pyramid is down to the efforts of people who have used Classic Rugby to generate interest in the game and to nurture its development.

The commitment of World Rugby and its predecessors is also significant. The experience of playing in a Rugby World Cup may be painful for some nations, but the structure which has emerged enables them to contest meaningful, competitive matches close to home.

Rugby's global expansion is being supported in a different way by Jason Leonard through the Atlas Foundation. His travels around the world as a top rugby player and a highly respected ambassador for the game have heightened Jason's awareness of the number of charities which have strong rugby connections and are prevented from operating effectively because of a lack of scale and profile as well as a shortage of funds. Jason has launched the Atlas Foundation to persuade his contacts in rugby and the corporate world to provide the resources which will help these charities make a real impact.

I am grateful to have the support of a true legend of world rugby for *Never Mind the Drop Goal*, and I am delighted to donate half of my royalties from the book to the Atlas Foundation.

Phil Ascough, 2015

Round 1

Highs – and Lows – from History

From an inaugural tournament in 1987 to one of the world's biggest international sporting festivals, the Rugby World Cup has made remarkable progress and created its own unique set of memories.

1   Which player, who has never scored a point at the Rugby World Cup, holds the record for number of appearances, with twenty-two from four tournaments?

2   Who presented the trophy at the end of the 1995 Rugby World Cup in South Africa?

3   Which player, who had been capped for Samoa in 1986, scored the first try of the first Rugby World Cup in 1987 – playing for New Zealand?

4   Which member nation of the International Rugby Football Board, as it was known at the time, was the first to lose a Rugby World Cup match to a non-member nation?

5 Which nation beat Scotland in the quarter-final in 2007 to reach the Rugby World Cup semi-final for the first time?

6 Which was the first stadium to host the Rugby World Cup final twice?

7 Which team lost all three pool games on its tournament debut in 2011 but ran in 3 tries against Australia?

8 Which was the first Rugby World Cup final to be settled in extra time?

9 Which Rugby World Cup final produced the most tries, and how many were scored?

10 Which soprano performed 'World in Union', the official song of the Rugby World Cup, when it was introduced at the 1991 tournament?

11 Which nation, ever-present at the Rugby World Cup, made the most of being drawn in a group with Romania

and Fiji in 1991 to reach the quarter-finals for the only time in its history?

12 Who are the only team to have contested a Rugby World Cup final without winning the trophy, having posted three defeats from three appearances?

13 Thretton Palamo became the youngest player to appear at the Rugby World Cup when he lined up for which nation in 2007, at the age of 19 years and 8 days?

14 Which nation faced the hosts in the opening matches of the Rugby World Cup tournaments in 1999, 2003 and 2007?

15 Which player, in 2007, became the first to score points in two Rugby World Cup finals?

The Winners – Australia

Australia was the first team to lift the William Webb Ellis Cup twice, but each of the previous winners will be quick to remind the Wallabies that it's been a while now. They've also hosted or co-hosted the tournament twice, although without the same success, and are without doubt one of the Rugby World Cup heavyweights. The Aussies have had their bad days, but opponents usually need to be on top of their game to counter their typically open and flowing style.

1 Which Australian became the first player to exceed 900 points in international rugby when he kicked 1 conversion and 5 penalties in defeat against England in the quarter-final in 1995?

2 Which player scored the only try of the game in Australia's Rugby World Cup final victory over England in 1991?

3 Australia failed to top their pool in 2011 after losing to which Six Nations team in their second match?

4 Which opponents knocked out Australia at the semi-final stage in the first Rugby World Cup, winning 30–24 in Sydney?

5 Which team was the only one to prevent the Wallabies from scoring a try in Australia's Rugby World Cup-winning campaign of 1991?

6 Who was the only player to score in each of Australia's matches as they won their second Rugby World Cup in 1999?

7 In 1995 which team was the first to beat Australia in a pool match at the Rugby World Cup, winning 27–18 in Cape Town?

8 Which player holds the record for the number of appearances for Australia at the Rugby World Cup, with twenty between 1995 and 2007?

9 Which former Brisbane Broncos rugby league player scored Australia's first try as they hosted the 2003 Rugby World Cup?

10 Which East European nation – a participant in every Rugby World Cup – provided the opposition for Australia's first match in its triumphant 1999 campaign?

11 Which Aussie kicked 4 penalties in defeat against England in the 2003 final to take his points total to 100 for his only Rugby World Cup tournament?

12 In the 1987 Rugby World Cup, against which opponents did David Codey become the first Australian to be sent off in a Test match?

13 Australia played four of their five 1987 Rugby World Cup matches in Sydney. Which city hosted the other one?

14 Which player's try against Canada at the 2007 Rugby World Cup gave him an Aussie record total of 11 from three tournaments, one more than David Campese?

15 Which nation has inflicted the greatest number of defeats on Australia at the Rugby World Cup, with three since the tournament began?

The Winners – England

Such is the fervour for sporting success in England that the rugby team carried the weight of frustration from fans of failed performers in football, cricket and even tennis when they lost the 1991 Rugby World Cup final. Sir Clive Woodward's heroes of 2003 set new standards in every aspect of the game, and while their success will have left no one under any illusions about England's place in world rugby, it demonstrated what can be achieved and how positively the nation will respond.

1   England hold the record for the most drop goals at the Rugby World Cup with 20 from forty matches. Jonny Wilkinson landed 14 and Rob Andrew 5, but who scored the other one?
2   With which team did England's Rugby World Cup-winning captain, Martin Johnson, spend his entire club career?

3 Which England scrum-half, who featured in five matches during the 1995 Rugby World Cup, was born in the Welsh town of Crickhowell?

4 Which team became the first opponents to keep a clean sheet against England when the sides met in the pool stage of the 2007 Rugby World Cup?

5 Who were the first opponents to beat England after their 2003 Rugby World Cup triumph?

6 England are one of the few teams to reach a Rugby World Cup final having lost a match earlier in the tournament. Which team beat them in the pool stage of the 1991 tournament?

7   Which player passed Philippe Sella's record of 111
    international caps when he came off the bench for
    England in their semi-final win over France in 2003?
8   Which prop came home from the 2011 Rugby World
    Cup after injuring his shoulder in England's opening game
    against Argentina – a fixture which would be the last of
    his forty Tests for his country?
9   Which England player made it into the pages of *New
    Musical Express* after releasing *Where We Go From
    Here*, an album of sixteen songs written while he was
    recovering from injury in 2009?
10 Which nation has England never beaten at the Rugby
    World Cup in three attempts?

11 Which player scored 5 of England's 17 tries as they beat Uruguay 111–13 in the pool stage of the 2003 Rugby World Cup?

12 Which is the only Six Nations team never to have faced England at the Rugby World Cup?

13 Which Pacific Island nation did England face in the quarter-final play-off after failing to win their pool at the 1999 Rugby World Cup?

14 Which rival from the home nations ended England's 1987 Rugby World Cup hopes at the quarter-final stage?

15 Which player was the only member of the England squad to play every minute of the victorious 2003 Rugby World Cup campaign?

Round

4

The Winners – New Zealand

Hosts twice and winners on each occasion, New Zealand are increasingly desperate to taste Rugby World Cup success away from home. For the All Blacks, runners-up are the first losers, and semi-final exits a disaster, so don't even think about the quarter-final defeat of 2007! They bounced back from that to win the Cup four years later, and they dominate the tournament's team and individual scoring records. But overall – whisper it – New Zealand's Rugby World Cup record is a bit of a mixed bag.

1   Which player set a record for the highest Rugby World Cup score by an individual, with 45 points for New Zealand against Japan in 1995?

2   David Kirk lifted the Webb Ellis Cup for New Zealand in 1987 after which player, who had been appointed captain, missed the tournament through injury?

3 What was the nickname of Va'aiga Tuigamala, who played at Rugby World Cup tournaments for New Zealand and then Samoa either side of a successful rugby league career with Wigan?

4 New Zealand's earliest exit from the Rugby World Cup came in the quarter-finals in 2007. Who beat them?

5 Which star of New Zealand's 1987 Rugby World Cup-winning side returned to the tournament as coach of Italy in 2002 and Japan in 2007?

6 Which team was the first to beat New Zealand at the Rugby World Cup?

7 In the amateur age, New Zealand full-back John Gallagher was back at work in Wellington the day after winning the Rugby World Cup in 1987. What was his day job?

8 Which player crossed the line to claim 4 tries in his only Rugby World Cup appearance as New Zealand beat Canada in 2011?

9 New Zealand have never lost a pool match at the Rugby World Cup. Which team pushed them the closest, losing by 6 points in 1991?

10 Which player missed two matches because of a nagging foot injury but was there when it mattered to lead New Zealand in five of their seven games at the 2011 Rugby World Cup?

11 Which flying winger scored 2 tries in the first 12 minutes to set New Zealand on the way to a 108–13 victory over Rugby World Cup newcomers Portugal in the 2007 tournament?

12 Which record was set by Brad Thorn when he appeared for New Zealand in the 2011 Rugby World Cup final?

13 Which player kicked all 12 points for New Zealand in the 1995 Rugby World Cup final but missed the target with a drop goal attempt which would have secured victory in the closing minutes of normal time?

14 Which player became the first to score 2 hat-tricks at the Rugby World Cup, with 3 tries against Japan in 1995 and 3 more against Italy in 1999?

15 Which player became the youngest to appear in a Rugby World Cup final when he lined up for New Zealand against South Africa in 1995?

The Winners – South Africa

South Africa have been making up for lost time since their belated admission to the Rugby World Cup and two successes from just five attempts have put them on a par with their fellow southern hemisphere powerhouse nations. But when they haven't been storming their way to the final, the Springboks have fallen in the last eight, the traditional intensity of their game giving way to a vulnerability which the most determined opponents have been able to exploit.

1 Who were the opponents for South Africa's first match at the Rugby World Cup?
2 Which was the first team to beat South Africa at the Rugby World Cup?
3 Who was the only South Africa player to appear in both of their Rugby World Cup final victories?

4 Which player, who was the most-capped Springbok when he retired in 2003, was a member of the Rugby World Cup-winning side in 1995 and captain of the team who defended the title four years later?

5 Which player was initially ruled out of the 1995 Rugby World Cup through injury but recovered to score 4 tries in the quarter-finals against Samoa and then held his place as South Africa won the trophy?

6 Which player scored in each of South Africa's first five games at the 1999 Rugby World Cup but sat out the third-place play-off and finished the tournament 3 points short of a century?

7 Who, in 2007, became the first South African to finish a Rugby World Cup tournament as top scorer?

8 Which two nations, each making their first appearance at the Rugby World Cup, found themselves in the same pool as South Africa for the 1999 tournament?

9 In 2011 which official became the second South African to referee a Rugby World Cup final?

10 South Africa hooker James Dalton was suspended for the rest of the 1995 Rugby World Cup after being sent off against which nation in the pool stage?

11 Which player, who shone during the Springbok successes of the late 1990s, played only two matches in the Rugby World Cup – scoring 11 points in the 1999 play-off win over the All Blacks, which was his last Test appearance?

12 Which South African finished the 2011 Rugby World Cup as the tournament's top scorer despite only playing five games as the Springboks exited at the quarter-final stage?

13 Which former player, who coached South Africa at the 1999 Rugby World Cup, returned to the tournament in 2011 as coach of Italy?

14 Against which nation did South Africa overhaul a 6-point deficit to win 17–16 in their opening pool match at the 2011 Rugby World Cup?

15 Who was the victorious captain when South Africa lifted the Rugby World Cup at their first attempt in 1995?

Round

6

The Rest – Argentina

The newest of the southern hemisphere's top-tier rugby nations is the only one not to have won the Rugby World Cup, and that's how it's likely to be for some time yet. But while Argentina have grown in stature – their only defeats at the last two tournaments have come against former winners – history shows they've only really found their scoring touch against Namibia and Romania.

1 Although recognised as a force in rugby union now, Argentina won only one match in their first three Rugby World Cup tournaments. Which nation did they beat?

2 Which Argentina player scored a total of 102 points at the 1999 Rugby World Cup and was awarded the Golden Boot?

3 Which opponents did Argentina overcome in 2014 to record their first win in the SANZAR Rugby Championship?

4 Who kicked 28 points for South Africa as they romped to a record 73–13 victory over Argentina in the 2013 Rugby Championship?

5 Against which team did Argentina score 29 unanswered points at the 1999 Rugby World Cup to turn a 13-point half-time deficit into a 32–16 win?

6 Which player, who was captain of Argentina for more than half of his sixty-six Tests, led his nation in its three 1987 Rugby World Cup matches at the age of 35?

7 Which nation set the record for the highest score against Argentina at the Rugby World Cup, winning 47–26 in Dublin in 1999?

8 What is the nickname of the Argentina rugby union team?

9 At which Rugby World Cup did Argentina record six wins, double their highest number of victories at any other edition of the tournament?

10 Which player holds the record for the number of points scored for Argentina at the Rugby World Cup?

11 Against which team did Argentina record their biggest victory at the Rugby World Cup, winning 63–3 in September 2007?

12 Pedro Sporleder became the first Argentina player to receive a red card at the Rugby World Cup when he was sent off at the 1991 tournament during a match against which opponents?

13 Against which team did Argentina score 4 tries in a pool match at the 1995 Rugby World Cup, yet still lose the game as they ended the tournament with three straight defeats?

14 Argentina scored only 4 tries at the 1991 Rugby World Cup. Which player scored 3 of them?

15 Which nation did Argentina play in their first Rugby World Cup match in 1987 and then avoid until the draw paired them together for the 2015 tournament?

The Rest – France

It says everything about the standard and intensity of the northern hemisphere competition that the Six Nations have been represented in six out of seven Rugby World Cup finals, but fallen short in all but one of them.

France can claim to have been particularly unfortunate on some occasions, but have also been outclassed on others. The scale of opportunities missed is demonstrated by the fact that France have played more matches at the Rugby World Cup than England, appeared in more finals and contested more semi-finals. All they have to do now is win it.

1 Which legend of French rugby played his last Test for Les Bleus in the quarter-final defeat by England at the 1991 Rugby World Cup?

2 Which nation inflicted a double defeat on France in 2007, beating the hosts in the pool stage and again in the play-off for third place?

3 Which record was set by Jean-Marc Doussain when he came on to the field for France in the 2011 Rugby World Cup final?

4 Which Frenchman, who scored 2 tries for his country at the first Rugby World Cup, coached Italy at the 2007 tournament?

5 Which coach took France from the wooden spoon spot at the 1999 Five Nations to the Rugby World Cup final in November that year?

6 Which player holds the record for the most points scored for France at the Rugby World Cup, with 124 from his nine appearances in the tournament?

7 Who are the only top-tier nation to concede more than 50 points against France in a match at the Rugby World Cup?

8 France's record of six consecutive wins at the Rugby World Cup began with victory over England in 1995 and ended with defeat against which nation at the 1999 tournament?

9 France have reached the last four of the Rugby World Cup at every attempt except 1991, when which opponents beat them in the quarter-finals?

10 Which player missed France's opening Rugby World Cup match in 1987 but finished as their top scorer for the tournament, scoring 4 tries and kicking with deadly accuracy to amass 53 points?

11 In a low-scoring tournament, France set the record for the highest number of tries in a match at the 1991 Rugby World Cup with 6 against which pool stage opponents?

12 Which Six Nations rivals did France meet for the first time at the Rugby World Cup when they contested a semi-final in 2011?

13 France opened their 2007 Rugby World Cup campaign as hosts at the Stade de France, but in which stadium did they end with defeat in the play-off for third place?

14 Against which opponents do France have their best Rugby World Cup record, with four victories from four meetings?

15 Which Six Nations opponents had France avoided at the Rugby World Cup – until they were drawn in the same pool for the 2015 tournament?

Round

8

The Rest –
Ireland

Ireland have been known to spring the occasional shock
against the most serious Rugby World Cup contenders – but
usually in the autumn internationals! Their history in the
actual tournament is of straightforward wins over nondescript
opposition followed by heroic failure when it comes to the
crunch against the top sides in the knockout stages. But they've
never faced England in the tournament, and maybe that's what it
would take to kick-start a drive beyond the quarter-finals.

I Which player kicked 2 conversions which made the
   difference as Ireland laboured to a 14–10 win over
   Georgia in a pool game at the 2007 Rugby World Cup?

2 A last-gasp try by which player broke Irish hearts in the
   quarter-final of the 1991 Rugby World Cup and sealed
   victory for Australia by 1 point?

3 Which nations took the top two pool places at the 2007 Rugby World Cup, leaving Ireland in third place and consigned to their earliest exit from the tournament?

4 Which player kicked 3 conversions and a penalty as Ireland edged out Wales 24–23 in a pool game at Johannesburg in the 1995 Rugby World Cup?

5 Which nation did Ireland beat for the first time in five Rugby World Cup meetings in Auckland during the 2011 tournament?

6 Which side won a quarter-final clash in Melbourne in 2003 to deny Ireland a first Rugby World Cup meeting with England in the last four?

7 Which Belfast-born wing, who played more than forty Tests, scored 2 tries in Ireland's last Rugby World Cup clash with Canada – a 46–19 victory at the first tournament in 1987?

8 Which player, who featured in twenty-five Tests for
   Ireland, scored 6 tries at the 1991 Rugby World Cup, with
   4 of them coming in one match against Zimbabwe?

9 As co-hosts of the 1991 Rugby World Cup, Ireland played
   three of their matches in Dublin, but where was the
   venue for their other fixture, a pool-stage defeat against
   Scotland?

10 Eight different players scored tries as Ireland romped to a
   62–12 victory at the 2011 Rugby World Cup against which
   nation making their debut in the competition?

11 After coaching Ireland at the Rugby World Cup in 2003
   and 2007, which nation did Eddie O'Sullivan take to the
   tournament in 2011?

12 Noel Mannion played only one Rugby World Cup match
   for Ireland, scoring 2 tries in a 32–16 victory over which
   nation in 1991?

13   Which centre, whose fifty-six Tests included one for
     the Lions in Australia, made his mark on the first Rugby
     World Cup with a hat-trick of tries for Ireland in their
     only meeting at the tournament with Tonga?

14   Which former captain of the British and Irish Lions
     retired from playing the year before the first Rugby
     World Cup but led Ireland to the tournament as coach
     in 1991?

15   Which player set the Irish record for the number of tries
     at one Rugby World Cup tournament, touching down
     5 times in three games at the 2011 tournament?

Round 9

The Rest – Italy

Each of the Six Nations has graced at least the quarter-final stage of the Rugby World Cup, terrified or even bettered opposition of the highest standard and set new standards for the game in the northern hemisphere – except Italy. The Azzurri's only record of note since their admission to the Six Nations in 2000 is 'winners' of the most wooden spoons, but the mixed standard at the Rugby World Cup offers some comfort. In recent years the expanded tournament has enabled Italy to record two wins in their pool games, albeit against teams in our Also-Rans section.

1 Which fly-half played two Tests for his native Argentina before starring for Italy and representing his adopted nation at three Rugby World Cup tournaments?

2 Defeat against which Pacific Island nation, coupled with heavy losses against England and the All Blacks, brought Italy's only winless Rugby World Cup in 1999?

3 Which star of Italian rugby scored his first Test try against Canada at the 2003 Rugby World Cup and had progressed to captain his side by the time he scored 2 more at the 2011 tournament?

4 Which Six Nations opponents did Italy face for the first time at the Rugby World Cup in their final pool game in 2011?

5 Which team scored a total of 101 points in their first two Rugby World Cup meetings with Italy – and then doubled their tally by winning the third match 101–3?

6 Italy's record win at the Rugby World Cup came at Trafalgar Park, Nelson, in 2011 against which team competing in their first tournament?

7   Which veteran of Italian Test rugby scored his only Rugby World Cup try as his side beat Portugal 31–5 in the 2007 tournament?

8   Italy won two pool games at the Rugby World Cup for the first time in 2003 when they beat which nations who have competed at every tournament?

9   Which player was on the scoresheet for Italy in each of their three Rugby World Cup defeats to England in 1991, 1995 and 1999?

10 Which player set a record for the most points scored by an Italy player at a Rugby World Cup when he kicked 14 penalties and 4 conversions to reach 50 at the 2003 tournament?

11 Who became the only player to score a try for Italy in every match at a Rugby World Cup when he touched down in all three of his side's games in the 1995 tournament?

12 Which is the only nation to have been beaten twice by Italy at the Rugby World Cup, losing 9–30 in 1991 and 10–27 in 2011?

13 In 1995 which player became Italy's leading Rugby World Cup tryscorer with a total of 5 tries spread across three separate tournaments?

14 Which Italian made a record fourteen Rugby World Cup appearances for his country and scored a try in the last of them, a defeat against Scotland in 2007?

15 Which player, whose rugby league clubs included Warrington Wolves and Leeds Rhinos, switched codes and kicked 3 conversions and 3 penalties as Wales beat Italy in 2003 in the only Rugby World Cup match between the sides?

Round

10

The Rest – Scotland

A total of twenty-five nations have competed at the Rugby World Cup and, remarkably, Scotland have played against twenty of them. Inevitably, such a fixture schedule can skew their win record a little; they've achieved nineteen victories from thirty-three games, many against the likes of Georgia, Portugal and Spain, but none against any finalists.

Scotland have pushed the top teams to the limit and always avoided embarrassment, but without quite being able to complete the job. Their performance at the 1991 tournament is a classic case of what might have been.

I   Which stalwart of Five Nations and Lions rugby kicked 14 conversions in his last World Cup in 1995 to take his total from three tournaments to 39, a record for an individual?

2 Scotland's best finish at the Rugby World Cup was fourth place in 1991. Which team beat them in the semi-final?

3 Which one of the other Six Nations has Scotland never faced at the Rugby World Cup?

4 Which former player, who coached the British and Irish Lions in 1989, 1993 and 1997, was Scotland's head coach at the Rugby World Cup in 1991 and 1999?

5 Which Scotsman kicked 6 penalties out of 6 to secure an 18–16 victory and deny Italy an unprecedented third win in the pool stage – and qualification for the 2007 Rugby World Cup quarter-finals?

6 Scotland recorded the first draw at the Rugby World Cup in their first match. Who were their opponents for the contest in Christchurch in 1987?

7 Which nation beat Scotland in five of the first six Rugby World Cup tournaments?

8 Who were the victims when Scotland completed their biggest Rugby World Cup win on home soil, a 48–0 victory at Murrayfield in 1999?

9 Scotland played their pool matches for the 2007 Rugby World Cup at Murrayfield and in which French city?

10 Which team, making their first appearance at the Rugby World Cup, progressed to the quarter-final in 1991, where they were beaten by Scotland?

11 Which wing scored 2 tries for Scotland in their only Rugby World Cup meeting with the United States, a 39–15 win in Brisbane in 2003?

12 In which year of the Rugby World Cup did Scotland fail to qualify for the quarter-finals for the first time?

13 After playing five matches at Murrayfield during the 1991 Rugby World Cup, to which stadium did Scotland have to travel to contest the play-off for third place?

14 Which member of a famous rugby-playing family scored 4 tries for Scotland at the Rugby World Cup, including 1 in each of the team's first two games in the 1991 tournament against Japan and Zimbabwe?

15 Which team from Scotland's 2015 Rugby World Cup pool is the only one to have beaten them previously in the history of the tournament?

The Rest – Wales

Wales have famously humbled some of the biggest names at the Rugby World Cup, yet they have also slumped to embarrassing defeats against emerging nations. They've swept all before them in progressing to the final four, on one occasion only denied progress to the final by the tightest of margins. But they've also failed to negotiate safe passage through the pool games on three occasions.

1 Which nation scored a try 4 minutes from time to pull off a shock win over Wales in the 2007 tournament and claim a place in the quarter-finals?
2 Which Welsh wing and captain boasts seventy-two caps for his country and seven Lions appearances – plus a Scrabble challenge of four vowels and only one consonant in his first name?
3 Which nation did Wales beat by just 1 point to seal their best Rugby World Cup placing in the third-place play-off of 1987?

4 Which player was the top tryscorer for Wales as they finished third at the 1987 Rugby World Cup, with all four scores coming in the same match against Canada?

5 Which nation was the first to fail to score in a Rugby World Cup match against Wales, conceding 9 tries in losing 66–0 at the 2011 tournament?

6 Which player scored the only try of the game when Wales and France met for the first time at the Rugby World Cup in Auckland in 2011?

7 Which Welsh referee officiated at the Rugby World Cup in 2007 and 2011, including the 2011 quarter-final between New Zealand and Argentina?

8 Which player scored a hat-trick of tries in his first Rugby World Cup match for Wales as they beat Namibia in 2011?

9 Which record was set by George North when he scored the first of his 2 tries for Wales against Namibia at the 2011 Rugby World Cup?

10 Which player scored the first Rugby World Cup hat-trick for Wales, with 3 tries in his only appearance in the tournament, against Tonga in 1987?

11 Which nation have inflicted the most defeats on Wales in Rugby World Cup matches, recording four straight victories after a Welsh win in the first tournament?

12 Against which nation at the 2007 Rugby World Cup did Wales score 5 tries but still lose the match?

13 Which player overtook Gareth Thomas's record of fourteen Rugby World Cup appearances for Wales when

he captained the side against Australia in their last match of the 2011 tournament?

14 Which player made six appearances for Wales at the 1987 Rugby World Cup before switching codes and playing more than 300 rugby league matches for Widnes, later resuming his international union career?

15 Who scored his first Rugby World Cup try against New Zealand in 2003 and went on to set a Wales record of 10 tries from the three tournaments in which he played?

Round 12

The Also-Rans

Fifteen lower-tier nations have appeared at the Rugby World Cup, often in humiliating fashion. They are: the United States, Zimbabwe, Ivory Coast, Canada, Namibia, Fiji, Georgia, Spain, Uruguay, Russia, Tonga, Portugal, Samoa, Romania and Japan. All you have to do is match the players listed below with the teams they represented. To make it easier, we've added a clue. But we've tried to avoid using too many names where the connection would be obvious.

1 Gareth Rees featured in the first four Rugby World Cups for this nation whose best finish was a quarter-final berth in 1991.

2 Eugene Jantjies played in 2007 and 2011 for this team, whose best result from four tournaments is a 32–17 defeat against Ireland in 2007.

3 Seremaia Bai featured in 2007 and 2011 for a nation who have reached the quarter-finals of the Rugby World Cup on three occasions.

4 Mamuka Gorgodze made his Rugby World Cup debut in 2007 at his side's second tournament.

5 This nation has been ever-present at the Rugby World Cup and Andy Miller featured in three of its games at the 2003 tournament.

6 This team has appeared at every Rugby World Cup and Cristian Petre played in each of its matches at the last three tournaments.

7 Brian Lima holds the record for individual appearances for this nation at the Rugby World Cup, having played at its historic first match at the tournament in 1991.

8   Pierre Hola played eight matches in 2003 and 2007 for this nation who have been Rugby World Cup regulars, but who failed to qualify in 1991.

9   Todd Clever made his Rugby World Cup debut in defeat against England at this nation's fifth tournament in 2007.

10 Victor Kouassi played all three matches for this nation at the only Rugby World Cup for which they qualified, in 1995.

11 Vasco Uva was captain for three of this team's four defeats when they appeared at their only Rugby World Cup in 2007.

12 Denis Simplikevich played the last two matches of this team's only Rugby World Cup in 2011, and scored a try in each of them.

13 Andriy Kovalenco kicked 5 penalties for this team on his
and their Rugby World Cup debut in 1999, but they lost
all three matches.

14 Diego Aguirre is this nation's record points-scorer at the
Rugby World Cup, with 30 from the team's two wins and
five defeats in 1999 and 2003.

15 Richard Tsimba scored 2 tries in 1987 and 1 more in
1991, but this team played six matches in total at the two
tournaments – and lost all of them.

Round 13

North Versus South

The development of the autumn internationals has added a new dimension to the debate about rugby's north-south divide, one which can't be matched by the summer tours. From the early days of southern teams travelling north and playing a couple of games, the top sides will now test themselves against high-calibre opposition every weekend for a month. And every four years it becomes almost a dress rehearsal for the following year's Rugby World Cup.

1 What is the name of the trophy which was introduced in 1999 and is contested by Australia and Ireland?

2 Which player kicked 6 penalties for the Irish as they beat Australia 18–9 in November 2002 to claim the trophy for the first time?

3 The Dave Gallaher Trophy, named after the All Blacks captain who was killed in Belgium during the First World War, is contested by New Zealand and which northern hemisphere side?

4 The autumn internationals are now established in the global rugby calendar, but which southern hemisphere team headed north in November 1988 for a three-match tour which saw them lose to England before beating Scotland and then Italy?

5 England inflicted a record defeat of 53–3 on which southern hemisphere team at Twickenham in November 2002?

6 Which is the only northern hemisphere nation to have beaten New Zealand at the Rugby World Cup?

7 Which player, who scored more than 1,000 Test points for Italy, produced the first of his 9 tries for the team in a defeat against South Africa in November 2001?

8 Which team beat Australia in November 2008 to deny the Wallabies, All Blacks and Springboks a clean sweep of victories over Six Nations opposition?

9 With Lansdowne Road closed for redevelopment, which Dublin stadium was the venue for Ireland's fixtures against New Zealand and Argentina in autumn 2008?

10 The James Bevan Trophy was introduced in 2007 to commemorate which milestone in the history of rugby between Wales and Australia?

11 Which New Zealand player reached 100 Test caps when he played for the All Blacks against England in November 2013?

12 Which France fly-half scored a total of 55 points in two Tests against New Zealand – the Rugby World Cup semi-final in 1999 and a French win in Marseille the following year?

13 Which player scored 2 tries for Australia in December 1984 as the Wallabies beat Scotland 37–12 at Murrayfield to complete a Grand Slam of victories over the four home nations?

14 Who scored a try in his eighty-seventh and final appearance for Wales as they were beaten by Australia in the only autumn international in 2011 to feature two top-tier nations?

15 Tries from Mark Taylor and Gareth Thomas earned Wales a famous first win over which touring team at the Millennium Stadium in June 1999?

The Global Games

With the Rugby World Cup a relatively recent innovation, it's a case of looking further back in history to explore the game's international pedigree. Rugby is now established in the programme for the Commonwealth Games, and the sevens format, which has proved such a big success, will also feature in the next Olympic Games. But some of the teams who pioneered the sport at those early Olympics have become prominent in international rugby, and some have even won the Rugby World Cup.

1 In which decade did rugby union last feature as a medal sport at the Olympic Games?
2 New Zealand won every game they played in the Commonwealth Games rugby union competition until tasting defeat against which team in the 2014 final?

3 Brazil, who have qualified for the 2016 Olympic rugby tournament as hosts, lost their only Rugby World Cup qualifier to which Caribbean nation in 1996?

4 Which nation has won the greatest number of Olympic gold medals for rugby union?

5 Which nation, in 1998, hosted the first Commonwealth Games to feature rugby union?

6 Which player, who won sixty-three Test caps for the All Blacks, starred as New Zealand won the inaugural Commonwealth Games rugby tournament?

7 Germany and Great Britain each sent a club side to contest the first Olympic rugby tournament in Paris in 1900, but the gold was won by a team selected from clubs from which nation?

8 Which East European nation made its rugby Olympic debut at the 1924 Games in Paris?

9   Which nation won rugby silver at the first two
    Commonwealth Games tournaments, but were beaten by
    England in the semi-finals in 2006?

10 Only two teams contested the Olympic rugby
    competition in London in 1908, with Great Britain losing
    to which opponents who would become fierce rivals?

11 The founder of the modern Olympic Games was also
    the man who introduced rugby to the schedule, but the
    sport was dropped after he stepped down from the
    International Olympic Committee. What was his name?

12 Australia beat Wales, South Africa beat Scotland, but
    which team beat England as the three home nations fell
    at the quarter-final stage of the 2014 Commonwealth
    Games rugby tournament?

13 Syd Middleton played Olympic rugby for Australia and also represented his nation in which event at the 1912 Games?

14 Which nation, where rugby sevens is popular, was suspended from the Commonwealth following a military coup and subsequently absent from the Commonwealth Games in 2010?

15 Which stadium in Glasgow hosted the rugby tournament at the 2014 Commonwealth Games?

Ahead of Their Time

The advent of the Rugby World Cup helped pave the way to professionalism, which in turn took rugby to new levels of media coverage, commercial clout and the global game which we enjoy today. But there will always be the debate in the background about what might have been if such opportunities had been available earlier. Which stars of the game from the days of quagmire pitches and grainy black-and-white television coverage might have shone at the Rugby World Cup, if only they'd had the chance?

1 Which legend of Welsh rugby, who retired in 1972, is the uncle of Craig and Scott Quinnell, who represented their nation at the 1999 Rugby World Cup?

2 Which man, who captained Ireland and made five tours with the British and Irish Lions, became one of a

handful of rugby players to feature in the BBC's Sports Personality of the Year awards, with third place in 1974?

3 Which player, christened William Henry but known by his nickname, played twenty-five Tests for England between 1974 and 1984, and accumulated a total of 240 points which included only 2 tries?

4 Which player captained New Zealand to their first Grand Slam tour of the British Isles in 1978, a year after having played in two Test wins over the touring British and Irish Lions?

5 Which scrum-half, who won fifty-three caps for Wales and ten more for the Lions, is still remembered most fondly by many rugby fans for his stunning try for the Barbarians against the All Blacks in 1973?

6 Instantly recognisable for his flowing blond locks, which player led France to two Grand Slams in the Five Nations and also to a first victory in New Zealand? On retirement he opted for the more sedate occupation of artist and painter.

7 This five-time tourist with the Lions also has a footnote in rugby history as the first replacement in an international match, taking the field for the injured Barry John in Pretoria in 1968. In total, he made twelve Lions appearances and sixty-nine for Ireland. What is his name?

8 Which brothers, who were inducted into the IRB Hall of Fame in 2011, played more than eighty Tests between them for France in the 1960s, including eighteen matches together?

9 Which veteran of thirty-four Tests for New Zealand retired two years before the first Rugby World Cup kicked off, but has made his mark on the tournament as a TV analyst with a talent for mischievous sound bites?

10 Hailed as one of the game's great scrum-halves and particularly effective when working in partnership with Phil Hawthorne, which Aussie played twenty-seven Tests, but was forced to retire through injury in 1968 at the age of 28?

11 One of the great Scottish full-backs, which player made fifty-one Test appearances for his country and a further nine on his three tours with the British and Irish Lions before retiring in 1982?

12 The first Five Nations Grand Slam since 1957 was one of the great achievements of this lock who captained

England on twenty-one occasions. Retiring through injury in 1982, he continued to serve the game behind the scenes and as a TV quiz show captain. What is his name?

13 This player stunned the rugby world when he retired at the age of 25, just three years before the first Rugby World Cup. He also stunned the home nations by scoring a try in every match as the Aussie tourists claimed a Grand Slam in 1984. What is his name?

14 South Africa's isolation from world sport denied many players the chance to appear at the Rugby World Cup. Which centre's hat-trick against England in 1984 stands out in a career of twenty-four caps which ended in 1992?

15 This player actually featured for Scotland at the 1987 Rugby World Cup, but only for a few minutes. Injury early in Scotland's first game against France ended his career in his forty-third Test. What is his name?

Round 16

Crunching Tackles

The Rugby World Cup is the toughest of competitions, so here's a demanding section which some might be tempted to side-step. Drawn from tournaments throughout the competition's brief history, but embracing some of the lesser-known teams, obscure events and remote qualifying stages, it's a set of questions to test the knowledge of the most ardent fan.

I   Efraim Sklar became the first referee from outside the Six Nations or the Tri Nations to take charge of a Rugby World Cup match when he officiated for New Zealand against the United States in 1991. Where was he from?

2   The quarter-finals of the first Rugby World Cup comprised the seven member nations of the International Rugby Football Board at the time and which other team?

3 Which edition of the Rugby World Cup saw the introduction of qualifying matches for all but the tournament hosts and the top three teams from the previous competition?

4 Three of the Six Nations faced play-offs after the pool stage of the 1999 tournament. Which one of them failed to progress to the quarter-finals?

5 Who was the first referee to officiate in the Rugby World Cup final twice, taking the whistle for the showpiece match in 1999 and 2003?

6 What was the on-field connection between the Rugby World Cup final of 2011 and the first match of the 2015 qualifying campaign between Mexico and Jamaica in 2012?

7 Which Caribbean nation lodged an expression of interest to host the 2019 Rugby World Cup, but became the first candidate to withdraw?

8 In which Australian town would you find the Dairy Farmers Stadium, venue for three matches at the 2003 Rugby World Cup?

9 Which player became the youngest to win a Rugby World Cup final when he lined up for South Africa in 2007?

10 Which of the four nations to have won the Rugby World Cup have never provided the tournament's individual top scorer?

11 Who was the first England player to score a hat-trick in a Rugby World Cup match, with three tries against Japan in 1987?

12 Which southern hemisphere nations met for the first time in the Rugby World Cup at the semi-finals stage in 2007?

13 In which year did New Zealand and South Africa set a record by contesting the first Rugby World Cup final to feature two southern hemisphere sides?

14 Which team holds the best winning record for matches between the southern hemisphere nations at the Rugby World Cup, with six victories from eight games in the first seven tournaments?

15 What was remarkable about the pool matches which brought together Canada and Japan at the 2007 and 2011 tournaments?

Easy Victories

If the last round was the sports quiz equivalent of facing New Zealand as they fly off the leash at Eden Park, this one is more akin to taking on Namibia in your own backyard. Perhaps the main difference is that you can't score 100 points in this section.

1 Which New Zealander became the first full-time coach of Wales from outside the country and led the team to top spot in their pool in the 1999 World Cup?

2 Diego Ormaechea of which nation became the oldest player to appear in a Rugby World Cup match at the age of 40 years and 26 days in the 1999 tournament?

3 Which is the most northerly of the 2015 Rugby World Cup venues?

4 Which member of England's backroom team from the 2003 Rugby World Cup coached Scotland at the 2011 tournament?

5 Which nation has provided the top tryscorer at the Rugby World Cup in four of the seven tournaments?

6 Which brothers, who played together in the 1995 Rugby World Cup, were the first siblings to appear in the same England team since 1938?

7 Who were the only hosts of a Rugby World Cup tournament to fail to reach the semi-finals?

8 Which player kicked 70 points in seven Rugby World Cup matches to become Ireland's top scorer at the Rugby World Cup until being overtaken by Ronan O'Gara?

9 In 1999 which team became the only one of the Six Nations to lose every pool game at a Rugby World Cup tournament?

10 Which former rugby union coach was appointed Director of Sport for Team GB in 2006 to help with preparations for the 2012 Olympic Games?

11 Which nation has reached the quarter-finals of the Rugby World Cup five times but never progressed as far as the semi-finals?

12 Who was the captain of the Australia side which won its first Rugby World Cup in England in 1991?

13 New Zealand's Rugby World Cup final victories have both come against which team?

14 Which of the four Rugby World Cup winners have played the fewest matches at the tournament?

15 Which Irishman, who represented his country more than 130 times, scored the last of his seven Rugby World Cup tries in victory over Italy at the 2011 tournament?

Match-Winners

The team with the most match-winners is, more often than not, the team which will win the match. The more gifted players you have, the more you can get away with others having an off day – whether it's a speed king whose burst of pace leads to the crucial try, the half-back whose sudden change of direction creates the vital opening, or the kicker who can put the ball between the posts again and again and again.

1 New Zealand legend Jonah Lomu ran right through which England player on his way to scoring 1 of his 4 tries in a 1995 Rugby World Cup semi-final?

2 Which player scored a drop goal in the second period of extra time to win the Rugby World Cup for South Africa in 1995?

3 Which player scored all the points for England as the holders battled to beat Australia 12–10 in the quarter-finals of the 2007 Rugby World Cup?

4 France held on for victory by 1 point over Wales in the semi-final of the 2011 Rugby World Cup thanks to 3 penalties out of 3 by which scrum-half?

5 Which player scored a try for England in the 2003 Rugby World Cup quarter-final to steady the ship as Wales threatened to pull off a shock victory?

6 Who was the only player to score in every match as New Zealand marched to Rugby World Cup glory in 1987?

7 Which player kicked the penalties which were crucial in helping England reach the 1991 Rugby World Cup final but were not enough to claim the title?

8 Which player was the only one to break the 100-point barrier at the 2007 Rugby World Cup, reaching a total of 105 and kicking South Africa to glory?

9   Diego Albanese scored a late try for which team to edge
     out Ireland in the quarter-final play-offs at the 1999 Rugby
     World Cup?

10   Which Frenchman out-scored everyone except Jonny
     Wilkinson in the 2003 Rugby World Cup with a haul
     of 101 points which included tries against Japan and
     Scotland?

11   Which player won the battle of the boot against
     Australia's Michael Lynagh to earn victory for Wales by
     1 point in the third-place play-off in 1987?

12   Which player made the difference with 2 tries as South
     Africa laboured to victory by just 5 points against a
     determined Tonga side in the pool games of the 2007
     Rugby World Cup?

13   A penalty by which fly-half gave New Zealand a crucial
     cushion in the 2011 Rugby World Cup final and enabled
     them to resist the French fightback?

14   Which player scored 2 tries to put Scotland in command
     against surprise package Samoa in the quarter-finals of
     the 1991 Rugby World Cup?

15   Which player kicked 8 penalties in the 1999 Rugby World
     Cup semi-final against South Africa and 7 more in the final
     against France to win the trophy for Australia?

Controversies

It says everything about the higher disciplinary standards within rugby that a section about Rugby World Cup controversies is more to do with issues behind the scenes than any crazy or distasteful antics on the pitch. So we'll do what we can with the few red cards that have been brandished, the occasional row over video replays and the bizarre goings-on with food poisoning and paying fines with swine!

1 Which unwanted record was set by Huw Jenkins while playing for Wales against New Zealand in their 1987 semi-final?

2 Which player missed three of New Zealand's matches at the 1991 Rugby World Cup because of his refusal to play on a Sunday for religious reasons?

3 Max Brito was playing for which nation at the 1995 Rugby World Cup when he became paralysed from a neck injury after a ruck collapsed in a match against Tonga?

4   A military coup threatened the participation of which
    nation in the 1987 Rugby World Cup?

5   Which nation claimed to have been snubbed in favour
    of inferior teams for the 1987 Rugby World Cup and
    responded by reaching the quarter-finals of the next two
    editions of the tournament?

6   Why were France fined £2,500 by the International
    Rugby Board after their 2011 final against New Zealand?

7   Which nation reportedly declined its invitation to
    compete in the 1987 Rugby World Cup because of
    South Africa's membership of the International Rugby
    Football Board?

8 Which nation had two players sent off in its Pool A defeat against South Africa during the 1995 tournament?

9 Which England player had a try controversially disallowed by the television match official in the 2007 Rugby World Cup final against South Africa?

10 Why did New Zealand captain Sean Fitzpatrick lead his players out of the celebration dinner after the 1995 Rugby World Cup?

11 Which nation reportedly fined its coach 100 pigs as a result of allegations concerning his attitude towards players at the 2011 Rugby World Cup?

12 Which player was at the centre of controversy in the 1991 tournament after his deliberate knock-on denied

England's Rory Underwood a tryscoring opportunity in the final?

13 What did All Blacks manager Colin Meads blame for causing the food poisoning that affected several members of his team before and during the 1995 Rugby World Cup final?

14 What was at the centre of the dispute which saw New Zealand miss out on co-hosting the 2003 Rugby World Cup?

15 Which player was controversially sent off by referee Alain Rolland as Wales battled to defeat by just 1 point against France in the 2011 Rugby World Cup semi-final?

Biggest Wins

It is a nonsense to suggest that there are no easy games in top-level sport – unless, of course, we accept that many games at the Rugby World Cup are not top level. The first tournament in 1987 produced a good few examples of top sides running in 60 or 70 points, and some of the scores since would appear to have been the real inspiration for the introduction of Twenty20 cricket.

1 What was noteworthy about New Zealand's 145–17 win over Japan in the 1995 World Cup?
2 The highest-scoring final saw Australia and France rack up a total of 47 points in 1999, but how many tries were scored in the match?
3 Which nation conceded the most tries in a match at the 1987 tournament against France and the most points in a match in the 1991 tournament against Ireland?

4 Which is the only top-tier nation to have conceded 100 points in a single match at a Rugby World Cup tournament?

5 Which player scored a hat-trick of tries and was one of nine different tryscorers when France beat Namibia 87–10 at the 2007 Rugby World Cup?

6 Which team set a record-winning margin at the Rugby World Cup when it beat Namibia 142–0 in 2003?

7 Who was the busy goalkicker when England ran in 13 tries against Tonga in 1999 on the first occasion that they topped 100 points at the Rugby World Cup?

8 Who scored a hat-trick of tries for South Africa as they opened their 2003 Rugby World Cup campaign with a 72–6 win over Uruguay?

9   Against which nation did Wales win 57–10 in 1995, 64–15 in 1999 and 72–18 in 2007?

10 Wales and South Africa shared the record for the number of tries in one match at the 2011 Rugby World Cup by touching down 12 times each against which nation?

11 Which hooker, who scored 5 tries for Ireland in Rugby World Cup matches, delivered 4 of them in one match – a 53–8 drubbing of the United States in the 1999 tournament?

12 Against which side did Iwan Tukalo score a brace of tries as Scotland won 60–21 at the 1987 Rugby World Cup and a hat-trick when the result was 51–12 at a second meeting in 1991?

13 Samoa have delivered their fair share of Rugby World Cup shocks, but which nation trounced them 60–10 in 2003 and 59–7 in 2007?

14 Which nation faced the fiercest Rugby World Cup baptism, losing its first match in its first tournament 89–0 against Scotland in 1995?

15 Which team have suffered the heaviest defeat among the former winners of the Rugby World Cup, beaten 36–0 by South Africa in 2007?

Top Scorers

Longevity is the key for any player making his mark among the Rugby World Cup's list of top scorers. The kickers lead the way, rewarded for their consistency match by match over three or four tournaments. At the other end of the scale, Marc Ellis's 6 tries in one match against a no-hoper helped him to joint top spot in the only tournament he ever played.

1 Against which nation did Marc Ellis score a record 6 tries in a match during the 1995 Rugby World Cup?

2 Which player holds the record for the highest total of points scored in Rugby World Cup games, with 277 from nineteen matches?

3 Which player set a record for the number of penalties kicked at a Rugby World Cup tournament, with 31 in 1999?

4 Which All Black was the top scorer at the 1987 Rugby World Cup, with a total of 126 points?

5   Which Frenchman scored 4 tries in the pool stages and
    kicked the rest of his 112 points to finish as top scorer at
    the 1995 Rugby World Cup?

6   Which player scored 7 tries at the 1995 tournament and
    8 more in 1999 to set the record for the number of tries
    by an individual at the Rugby World Cup?

7   In which year did the top three individual scorers at a
    Rugby World Cup tournament each achieve a century of
    points?

8   Gavin Hastings became the first player to kick
    8 penalties in a Rugby World Cup match when Scotland
    beat which nation in the pool stage of the 1995
    tournament?

9   Kurt Morath became the first player from outside the
    top-tier nations to break into the top three scorers at a

Rugby World Cup when he scored 45 points for which team in 2011?

10 Nicky Little is the top scorer at Rugby World Cups from outside the top-tier nations. For which team did he score 125 points?

11 In 2011 Chris Ashton of England and Vincent Clerc of France became the first northern hemisphere players to finish joint top tryscorers at a Rugby World Cup since Jean-Baptiste Lafond in which year?

12 Which player kicked a world-record 5 drop goals as South Africa beat England at the quarter-final stage in 1999?

13 Which South African equalled the record for the number of tries scored in a Rugby World Cup tournament with 8 in 2007?

14 Which Irishman finished the 1991 Rugby World Cup as top scorer, with 68 points from only four matches?

15 Who is the only player to finish in the top three scorers at three successive Rugby World Cup tournaments – 1987, 1991 and 1995?

Touchline Kicks

Another round of tough questions, the equivalent to those kicks from distance and with some difficult angles. In the main they call for concentration, experience of the big occasion and alertness to possible trickery. But with some the preferred approach might just be to have a go and hope for the best!

1 Which is the only team to have played at the Rugby World Cup finals and failed to score a try?

2 In addition to Wales, which current force in world rugby was beaten by Samoa in 1991 as the Pacific Islanders progressed to the quarter-final?

3 What was the face value of the coin produced by the Royal Mint to commemorate the 1999 Rugby World Cup?

4 Which record was set by Stephen Donald and François Trinh-Duc in the 2011 Rugby World Cup final?

5 According to Australia's management team, what was
  John Eales worried he would have to leave behind if
  defeat against Ireland had led to an early flight home for
  the Wallabies in 1991?

6 Which two players scored all the points in the 1995
  Rugby World Cup final, the first one to fail to produce
  a try?

7 Brad Thorn became the oldest player to win the Rugby
  World Cup in 2011 at the age of 36 years and 262 days.
  Which winner, from 2003, had previously held the record
  at 35 years and 100 days?

8 François Trinh-Duc's conversion in the 2011 final was
  the first successful attempt in the showpiece match since
  which Australian player kicked for glory in 1999?

9 Which nation was unsuccessful with its bid to host the 2007 Rugby World Cup?

10 Which referee turned down the offer of a gold watch from Louis Luyt, president of the South African Rugby Football Union, when the 1995 post-tournament dinner ended in controversy?

11 Which nation, host of an international rugby tournament for veteran players, won the North America Caribbean Rugby Association qualifying competition for the 2015 Rugby World Cup before losing to Confederación Sudamericano de Rugby winners Paraguay?

12 Which South American nation qualified for the 1999 Rugby World Cup for the first time after negotiating its way through a new repêchage system for teams beaten in the qualifying rounds?

13 Which nation withdrew its bid to host the 2019 Rugby World Cup and instead campaigned successfully to host the Rugby World Cup Sevens in 2013?

14 Mark Cueto and Chris Ashton each scored a hat-trick of tries as England beat which nation 67–3 in the 2011 Rugby World Cup?

15 Which player was England's top tryscorer in their victorious Rugby World Cup campaign of 2003?

Round

23

Front of the Posts

Perhaps harshly, Gavin Hastings will always be remembered for fluffing the kick in front of the posts which would have put Scotland back on terms with England in their 1991 Rugby World Cup semi-final. Hastings has since admitted that he was still feeling the effects of a heavy tackle when he attempted the penalty. But the kick should have been easy – even easier than some of these.

1 Which nation won a two-legged play-off against Russia to become the last team to qualify for the 2015 Rugby World Cup?

2 'One team, one nation' was the slogan behind which team, which made its Rugby World Cup debut in 1995?

3 In which city was Telstra Stadium, the venue for the 2003 Rugby World Cup final?

4   Frano Botica, a member of New Zealand's Rugby World
    Cup-winning squad in 1987, switched codes three years
    later and played more than 170 matches for which English
    rugby league club?

5   Tony Woodcock's try against France in 2011 was the first
    in a Rugby World Cup final since 2003, when which player
    touched down for England?

6   Which nation marked the semi-final of the 2011
    tournament by becoming the first to pass 2,000 points in
    the final stages of the Rugby World Cup?

7   What was introduced to the format of the 1999 Rugby
    World Cup after the pool stage, but discarded for
    subsequent tournaments?

8   Which coach was said to be on the brink of dismissal
    after New Zealand's quarter-final exit in the 2007 Rugby
    World Cup, but clung to the job and led the team to
    victory in 2011?

9   Who, in 2003, became the first rugby union player to be
    named BBC Sports Personality of the Year? Who came
    second?

10 Which name connects the Rugby World Cup trophy,
    a stadium in Johannesburg and a record-breaking
    tryscorer?

11 What nationality was Kerry Fitzgerald, the referee for
    four matches at the inaugural Rugby World Cup, including
    the first final?

12 Who coached Ireland at the 1999 Rugby World Cup and
    returned to the tournament with Wales in 2011?

13 Which Football League club recruited Sir Clive
Woodward to its management team after his departure
from his England rugby union role?

14 Which official, who served as referee in the 2007 Rugby
World Cup final and assistant referee in the 2011 final,
played three Tests for Ireland between 1990 and 1995?

15 Which player was Will Carling talking about when he
reportedly told journalists at the 1995 tournament: 'He is
a freak and the sooner he goes away the better!'?

Fields of Dreams

The imagination which the Rugby World Cup organisers have demonstrated in attracting some of the more obscure nations to participate in the tournament has yet to find its way into the hosting process. So far the tournament hasn't left the established nations, and in truth the financial and organisational demands placed on a host are such that the situation is unlikely to change. But there are some interesting venues mixed in with the rugby cathedrals of Twickenham, Newlands and the Millennium Stadium.

1 Which stadium in New Zealand hosted the opening game in the first Rugby World Cup in 1987?

2 Ashton Gate, a venue for the 1999 Rugby World Cup, is the home ground of which English Football League team?

3 Organisers of the 2011 tournament were reluctantly forced to move seven matches to other venues after an earthquake struck which New Zealand city?

4 How many nations collaborated to host the second Rugby World Cup in 1991?

5 What is the name of the stadium in Wales which has hosted fixtures in rugby league, football and horse racing, and was the venue during the 1999 Rugby World Cup for the match between Samoa and Japan?

6 Which stadium was the only venue outside France to host a match in the knockout stages of the 2007 Rugby World Cup?

7 Cross Green stadium in which Yorkshire town was the smallest venue for the 1991 Rugby World Cup?

8 Which nation was selected in 2009 to host the 2019 Rugby World Cup?

9 At which stadium did Wales play their matches during the 1991 Rugby World Cup?

10 In which French city would you find the Stade Velodrome, a venue for the Rugby World Cup in 2007?

11 Which other European nation challenged England for the right to host the 2015 Rugby World Cup?

12 Which famous stadium, now demolished, was Llanelli's venue for Rugby World Cup matches in 1991 and 1999?

13 Which Australian city hosted the semi-finals of the 2003 Rugby World Cup?

14 In which South African city did Australia begin their defence of the Rugby World Cup against the 1995 hosts?

15 Which of the venues for the 2015 Rugby World Cup has the highest capacity?

Highs – and Lows – from History

1 Jason Leonard.
2 Nelson Mandela.
3 Michael Jones.
4 Wales, beaten by Samoa in 1991.
5 Argentina.
6 Eden Park, Auckland.
7 Russia.
8 The 1995 final between South Africa and New Zealand.
9 1987, when four were scored.
10 Dame Kiri Te Kanawa.
11 Canada.
12 France.
13 The United States.
14 Argentina.
15 Jonny Wilkinson.

The Winners
– Australia

1 Michael Lynagh.
2 Tony Daly.
3 Ireland.
4 France.
5 Samoa.
6 Matt Burke.
7 South Africa.
8 George Gregan.
9 Wendell Sailor.
10 Romania.
11 Elton Flatley.
12 Wales.
13 Brisbane.
14 Chris Latham.
15 England.

<table>
<tr><td>Round</td><td rowspan="2"># The Winners
– England</td></tr>
<tr><td>3</td></tr>
</table>

Round 3

The Winners – England

1 Mike Catt.
2 Leicester Tigers.
3 Dewi Morris.
4 South Africa.
5 Ireland, in the Six Nations.
6 New Zealand.
7 Jason Leonard.
8 Andrew Sheridan.
9 Andrew Sheridan.
10 New Zealand.
11 Josh Lewsey.
12 Ireland.
13 Fiji.
14 Wales.
15 Lawrence Dallaglio.

The Winners – New Zealand

1 Simon Culhane.
2 Andrew Dalton.
3 Inga the Winger.
4 France.
5 John Kirwan.
6 Australia, in 1991.
7 A police officer.
8 Zac Guildford.
9 England.
10 Richie McCaw.
11 Joe Rokocoko.
12 He became the oldest player to appear in the final.
13 Andrew Mehrtens.
14 Jeff Wilson.
15 Jonah Lomu.

The Winners – South Africa

1 Australia, in 1995.
2 Australia, in 1999.
3 Os du Randt.
4 Joost van der Westhuizen.
5 Chester Williams.
6 Jannie de Beer.
7 Percy Montgomery.
8 Spain and Uruguay.
9 Craig Joubert.
10 Canada.
11 Henry Honiball.
12 Morné Steyn.
13 Nick Mallett.
14 Wales.
15 François Pienaar.

The Rest – Argentina

Round 6

1 Italy.
2 Gonzalo Quesada.
3 Australia.
4 Morné Steyn.
5 Samoa.
6 Hugo Porta.
7 France.
8 Los Pumas.
9 2007 in France.
10 Gonzalo Quesada.
11 Namibia.
12 Samoa.
13 Italy.
14 Martin Teran.
15 Fiji.

The Rest – France

1 Serge Blanco.
2 Argentina.
3 He became the first player to make his international debut in a Rugby World Cup final.
4 Pierre Berbizier.
5 Jean-Claude Skrela.
6 Thierry Lacroix.
7 Scotland.
8 Australia.
9 England.
10 Didier Camberabero.
11 Fiji.
12 Wales.
13 Parc des Princes.
14 Fiji.
15 Italy.

The Rest – Ireland

1 Ronan O'Gara.
2 Michael Lynagh.
3 Argentina and France.
4 Eric Elwood.
5 Australia.
6 France.
7 Keith Crossan.
8 Brian Robinson.
9 Murrayfield.
10 Russia.
11 The United States.
12 Japan.
13 Brendan Mullin.
14 Ciaran Fitzgerald.
15 Keith Earls.

Round 9 The Rest – Italy

1 Diego Dominguez.
2 Tonga.
3 Sergio Parisse.
4 Ireland.
5 New Zealand.
6 Russia.
7 Mauro Bergamasco.
8 Tonga and Canada.
9 Diego Dominguez.
10 Rima Wakarua.
11 Paolo Vaccari.
12 The United States.
13 Marcello Cuttitta.
14 Alessandro Troncon.
15 Iestyn Harris.

1 Gavin Hastings.
2 England.
3 Wales.
4 Ian McGeechan.
5 Chris Paterson.
6 France.
7 New Zealand.
8 Spain.
9 Saint Etienne.
10 Samoa.
11 Simon Danielli.
12 2011.
13 Cardiff Arms Park.
14 Scott Hastings.
15 South Africa.

The Rest – Wales

1 Fiji.
2 Ieuan Evans.
3 Australia.
4 Ieuan Evans.
5 Fiji.
6 Mike Phillips.
7 Nigel Owens.
8 Scott Williams.
9 He became the youngest tryscorer in the history of the tournament at 19 years and 166 days.
10 Glen Webbe.
11 Australia.
12 Fiji.
13 Gethin Jenkins.
14 Jonathan Davies.
15 Shane Williams.

The Also-Rans

1 Canada.
2 Namibia.
3 Fiji.
4 Georgia.
5 Japan.
6 Romania.
7 Samoa.
8 Tonga.
9 The United States.
10 Ivory Coast.
11 Portugal.
12 Russia.
13 Spain.
14 Uruguay.
15 Zimbabwe.

North Versus South

1 The Lansdowne Cup.
2 Ronan O'Gara.
3 France.
4 Australia.
5 South Africa.
6 France.
7 Diego Dominguez.
8 Wales.
9 Croke Park.
10 100 years of Test rugby between the sides.
11 Dan Carter.
12 Christophe Lamaison.
13 David Campese.
14 Shane Williams.
15 South Africa.

The Global Games

1 The 1920s, and 1924 to be precise.
2 South Africa.
3 Trinidad and Tobago.
4 The United States, with two.
5 Malaysia.
6 Jonah Lomu.
7 France.
8 Romania.
9 Fiji.
10 Australia.
11 Pierre de Coubertin.
12 Samoa.
13 Eights rowing.
14 Fiji.
15 Ibrox.

Ahead of Their Time

1 Barry John.
2 Willie John McBride.
3 Dusty Hare.
4 Graham Mourie.
5 Gareth Edwards.
6 Jean-Pierre Rives.
7 Mike Gibson.
8 André and Guy Boniface.
9 Murray Mexted.
10 Ken Catchpole.
11 Andy Irvine.
12 Bill Beaumont.
13 Mark Ella.
14 Danie Gerber.
15 John Rutherford.

1 Argentina.
2 Fiji.
3 1999.
4 Ireland.
5 André Watson.
6 The same referee officiated in both matches.
7 Jamaica.
8 Townsville.
9 François Steyn.
10 Australia.
11 Mike Harrison.
12 South Africa and Argentina.
13 1995.
14 Australia.
15 Both matches were drawn.

Easy Victories

1 Graham Henry.
2 Uruguay.
3 St James' Park, Newcastle.
4 Andy Robinson.
5 New Zealand.
6 Rory and Tony Underwood.
7 Wales, in 1999.
8 David Humphreys.
9 Italy.
10 Sir Clive Woodward.
11 Ireland.
12 Nick Farr-Jones.
13 France.
14 South Africa, who only competed from 1995.
15 Brian O'Driscoll.

Match-Winners

1 Mike Catt.
2 Joel Stransky.
3 Jonny Wilkinson.
4 Morgan Parra.
5 Will Greenwood.
6 Grant Fox.
7 Jonathan Webb.
8 Percy Montgomery.
9 Argentina.
10 Frédéric Michalak.
11 Paul Thorburn.
12 Ruan Pienaar.
13 Stephen Donald.
14 John Jeffrey.
15 Matt Burke.

Controversies

1 He became the first player to be sent off at a Rugby World Cup.
2 Michael Jones.
3 Ivory Coast.
4 Fiji.
5 Samoa.
6 For breaking a 'cultural ritual protocol' for advancing beyond the halfway line during the haka.
7 Soviet Union.
8 Canada.
9 Mark Cueto.
10 Because Louis Luyt, president of the South African Rugby Football Union, said the Springboks were the first 'true' world champions, having been absent from the first two tournaments.
11 Samoa.
12 David Campese.
13 Dodgy milk.
14 Ground signage rights.
15 Sam Warburton.

Biggest Wins

1 New Zealand became the first team to score more than 100 points in a match at the World Cup.
2 Two.
3 Zimbabwe.
4 Italy.
5 Vincent Clerc.
6 Australia.
7 Paul Grayson.
8 Joost van der Westhuizen.
9 Japan.
10 Namibia.
11 Keith Wood.
12 Zimbabwe.
13 South Africa.
14 Ivory Coast.
15 England.

Top Scorers

1 Japan.
2 Jonny Wilkinson.
3 Gonzalo Quesada.
4 Grant Fox.
5 Thierry Lacroix.
6 Jonah Lomu.
7 2003.
8 Tonga.
9 Tonga.
10 Fiji.
11 1991.
12 Jannie de Beer.
13 Bryan Habana.
14 Ralph Keyes.
15 Gavin Hastings.

Touchline Kicks

1 Spain.
2 Argentina.
3 £2.
4 It was the first final in which two replacements scored points.
5 His dry-cleaning.
6 Joel Stransky and Andrew Mehrtens.
7 Jason Leonard.
8 Matt Burke.
9 England.
10 Derek Bevan.
11 Bermuda.
12 Uruguay.
13 Russia.
14 Romania.
15 Will Greenwood.

Front of the Posts

1 Uruguay.
2 South Africa.
3 Sydney.
4 Wigan.
5 Jason Robinson.
6 New Zealand.
7 Quarter-final play-offs.
8 Graham Henry.
9 Jonny Wilkinson won and Martin Johnson came second.
10 Ellis.
11 Australian.
12 Warren Gatland.
13 Southampton.
14 Alain Rolland.
15 Jonah Lomu.

Fields of Dreams

1 Eden Park, Auckland.
2 Bristol City.
3 Christchurch.
4 Five – England, France, Ireland, Scotland and Wales.
5 The Racecourse Ground, Wrexham.
6 The Millennium Stadium.
7 Otley.
8 Japan.
9 Cardiff Arms Park.
10 Marseille.
11 Italy.
12 Stradey Park.
13 Sydney.
14 Cape Town.
15 Wembley Stadium.

If you enjoyed this book, you may also be interested in …

978 0 7509 5842 4
£6.99

978 0 7524 9764 8
£6.99

978 0 7509 5468 6
£7.99

Visit our website and discover thousands of
other History Press books.

www.thehistorypress.co.uk